Decorate the beautiful hot-air balloons.

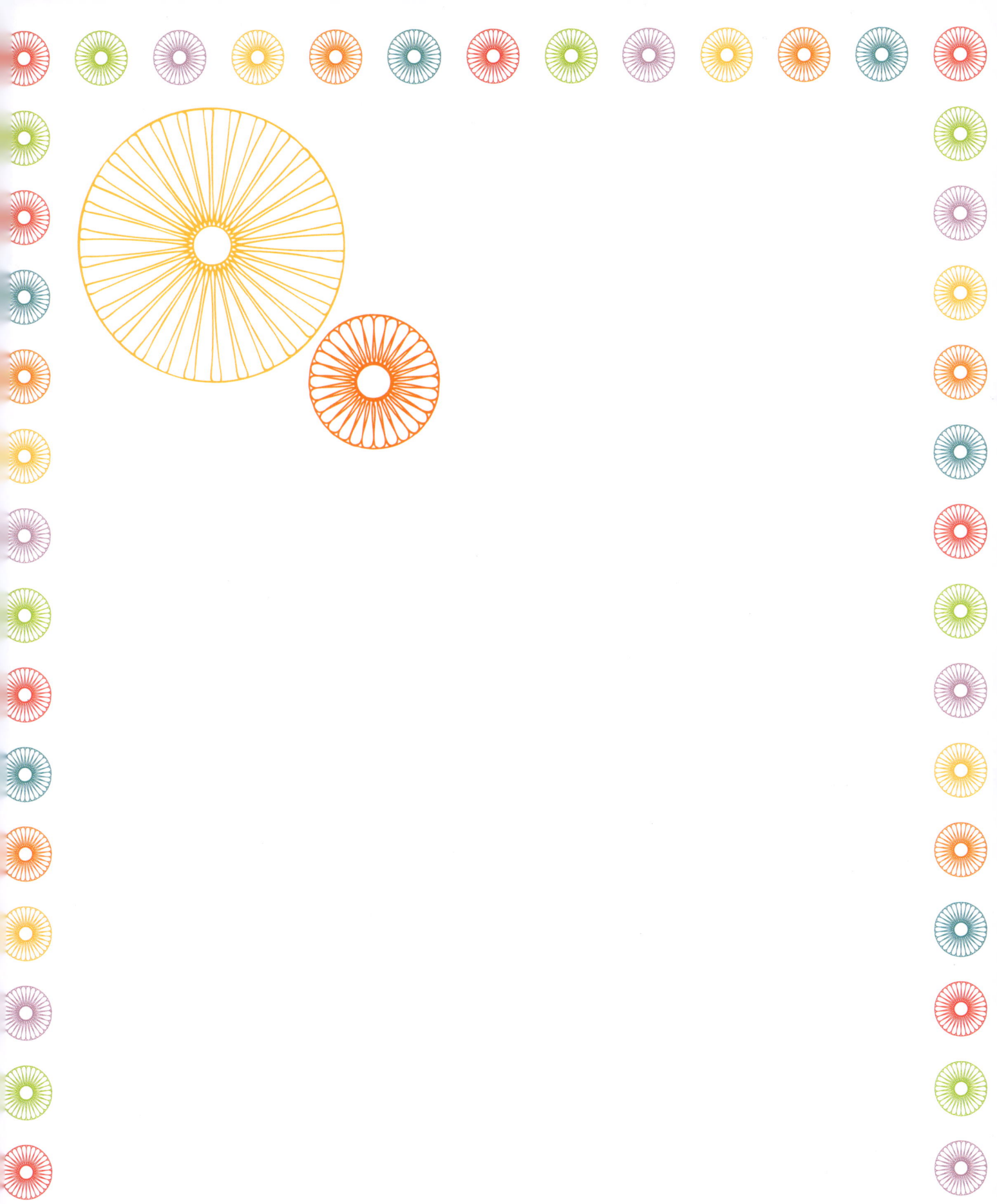

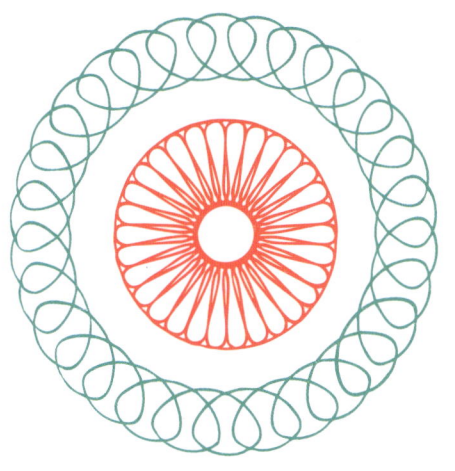

Create spiro ripples in the pond.

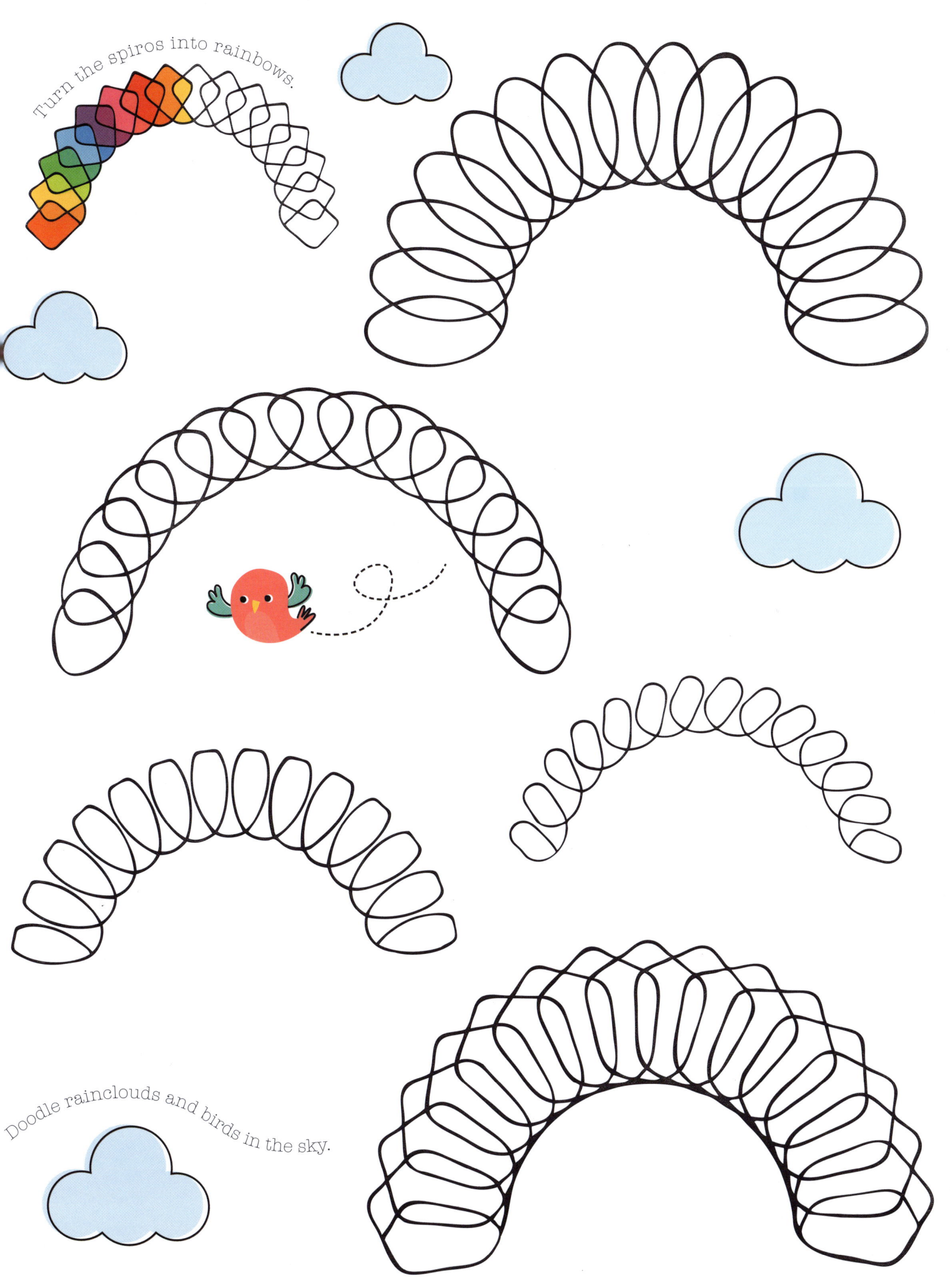

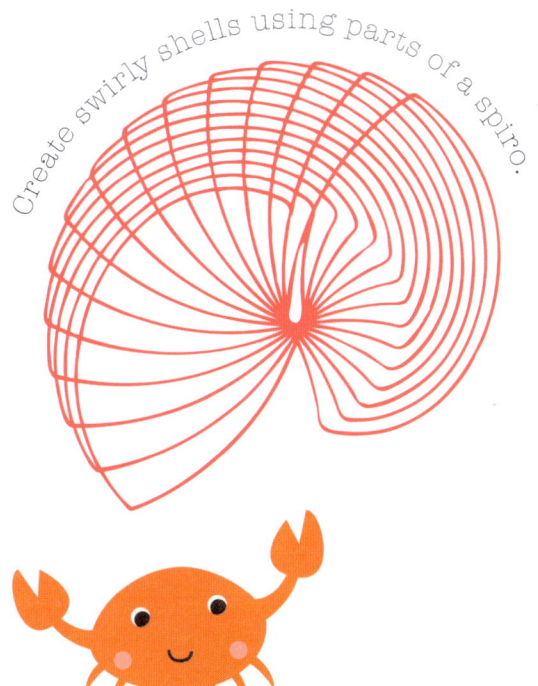

Create swirly shells using parts of a spiro.

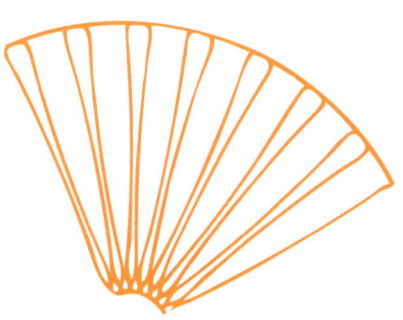

Doodle more cute crabs.

Add doodles and spiros to create gorgeous bags.

Fill the flower with pretty shades.

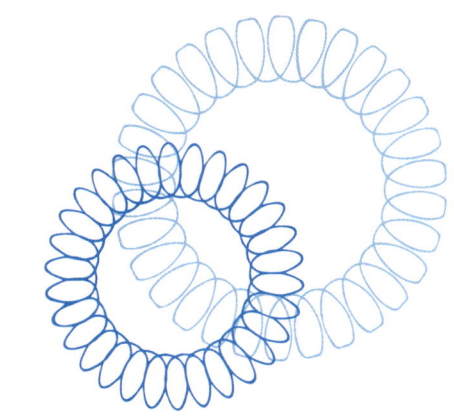
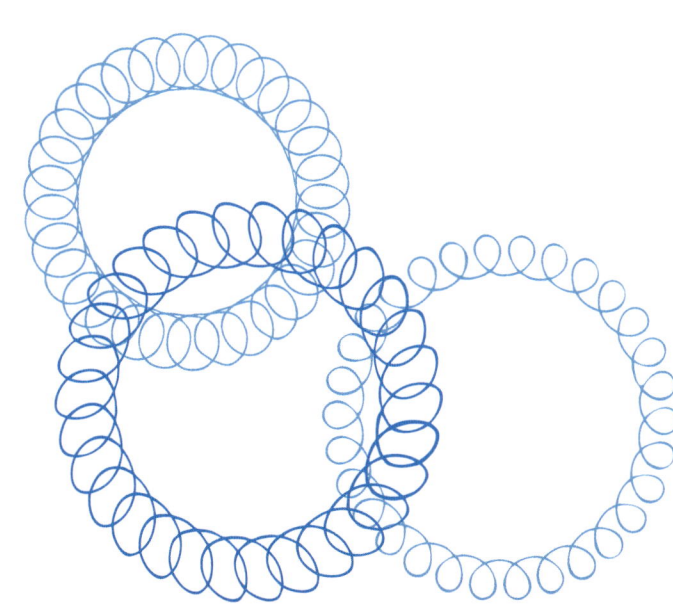

Decorate the giant butterfly wings.

Create a fantastic firework display.

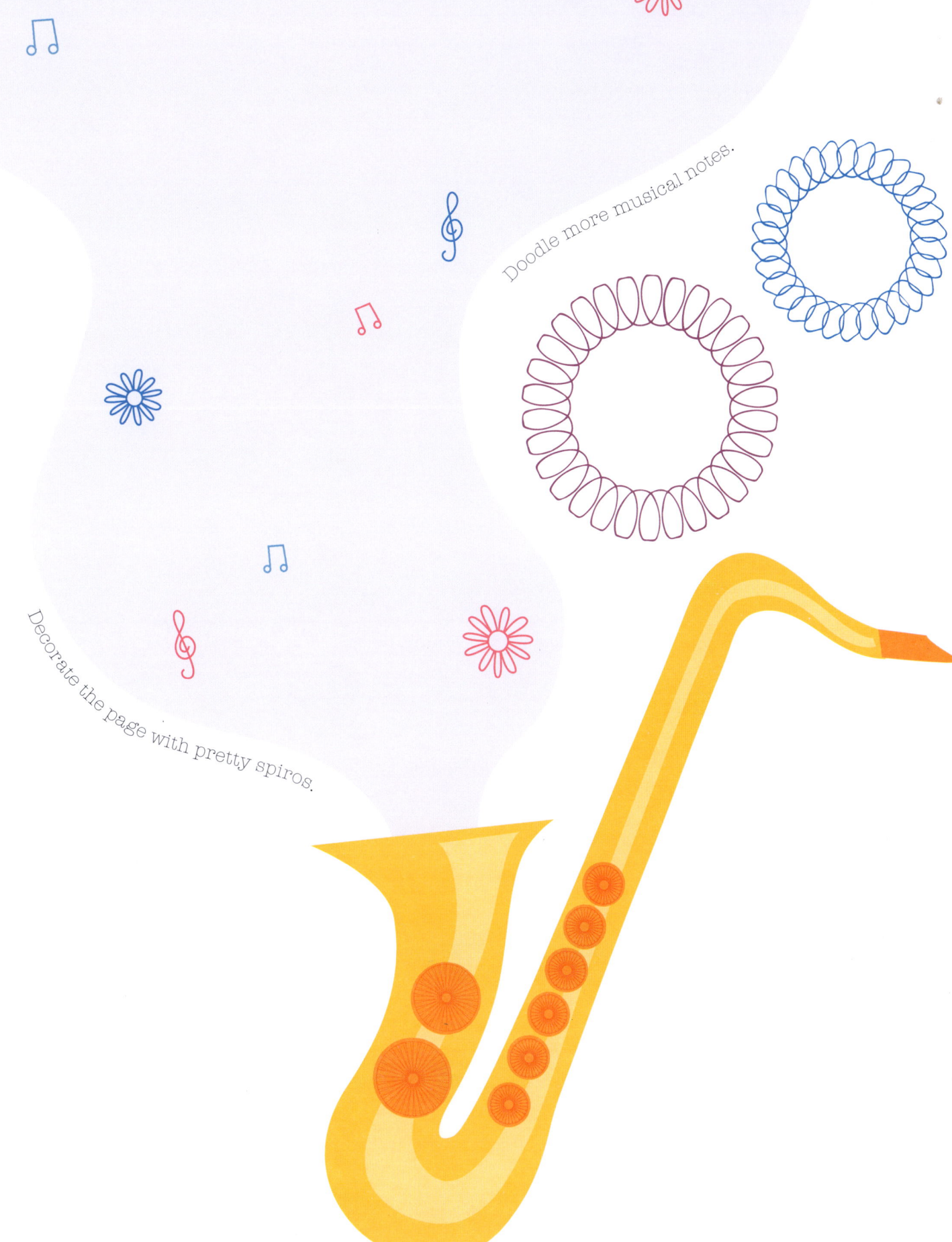

Doodle more musical notes.

Decorate the page with pretty spiros.

Create pretty spiro petals.

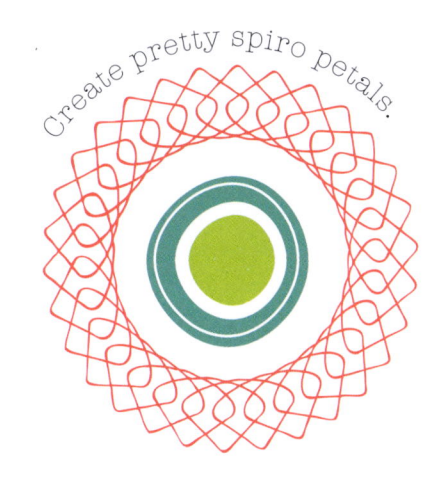

Spiro more floating jellyfish.

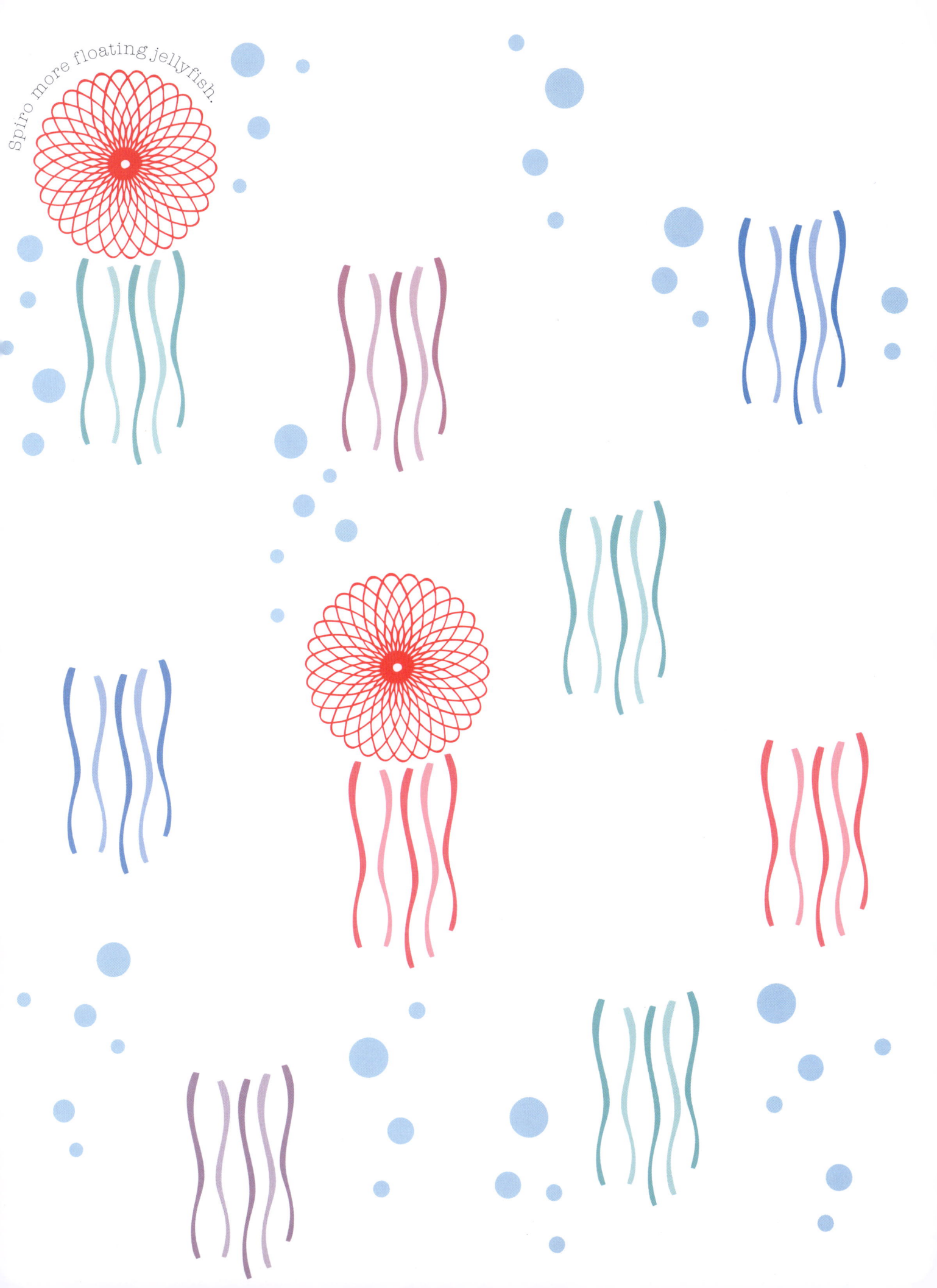

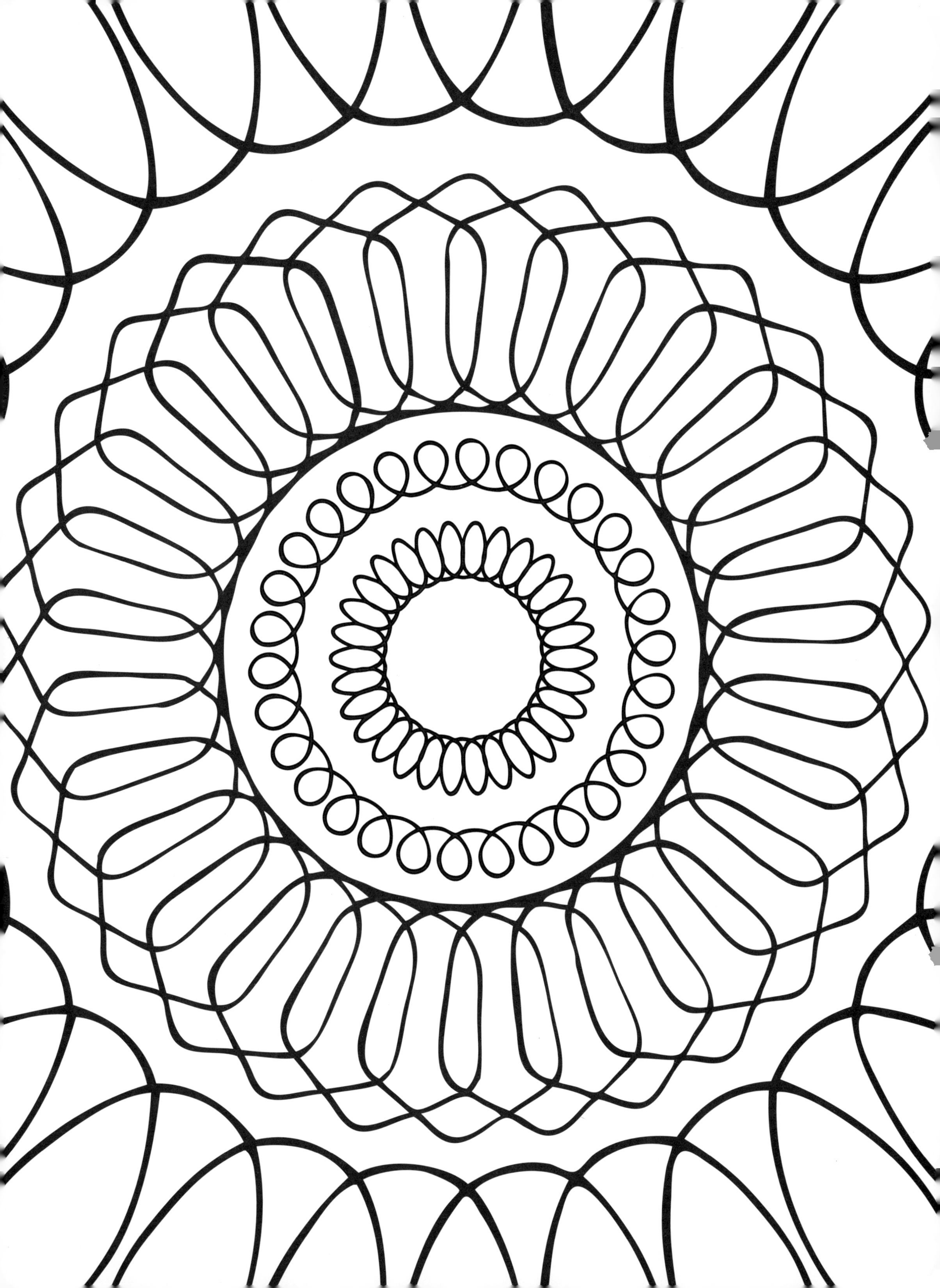

Create more spiro sweet treats.

Turn your spiros into cute animals.

Fill this page with delicious spiro food.

Make fabulous feathers for the chicks.

Fill the vase with pretty flowers.

Doodle details to create spiro bugs.

Draw more beautiful dancers.

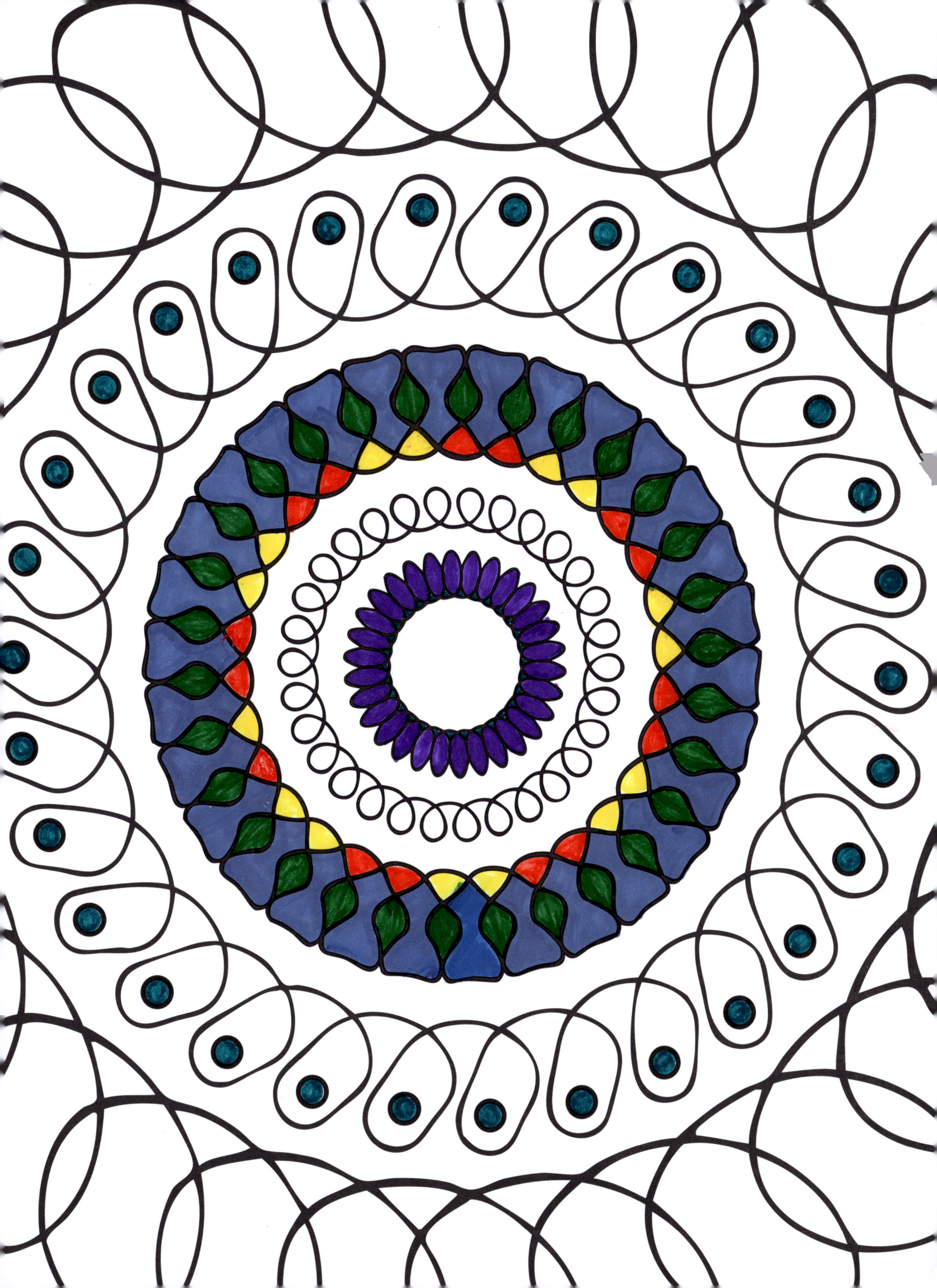

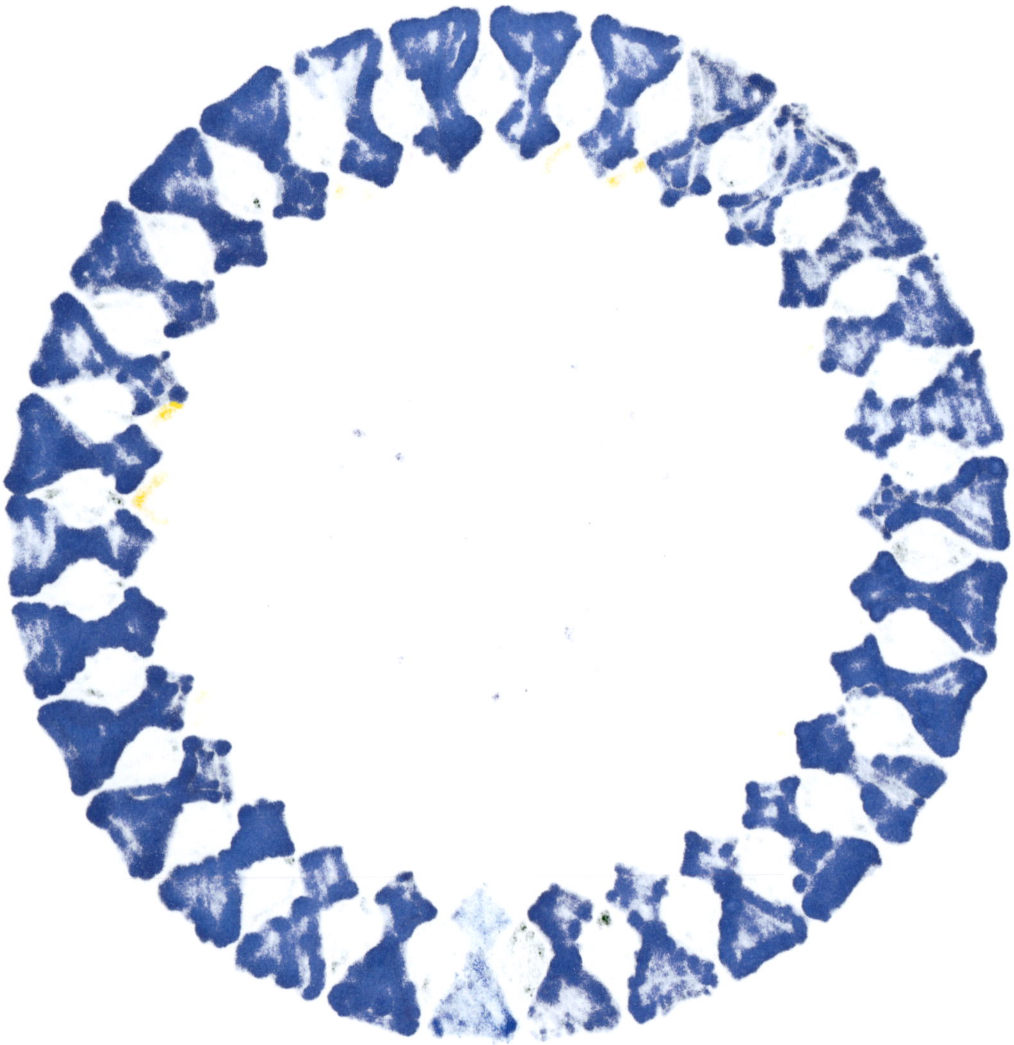

Add details to turn the spiros into perfume bottles.

Fill this shelf with spiro perfume bottles.

Fill the page with adorable spiro pets.

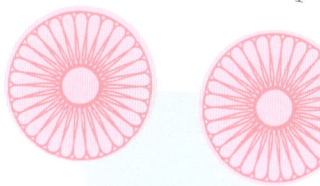

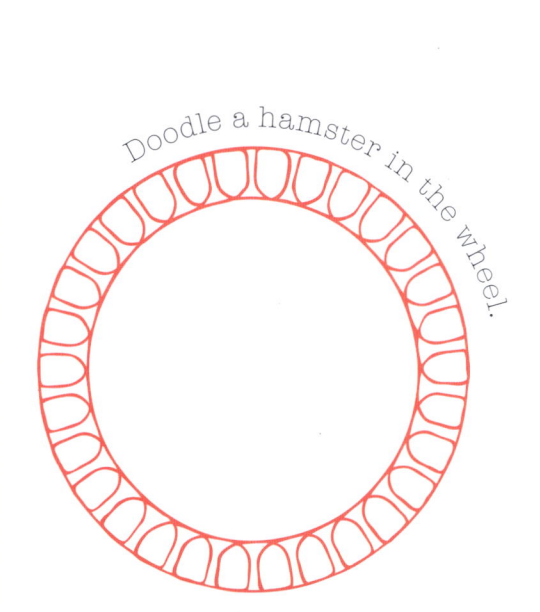

Doodle a hamster in the wheel.

Shade your spiros to make beautiful patterns.

Create perfect petals.

Fill the page with flowers.

Open a spiro hair salon.